EX CATHEDRA

XXIV

PETER JOANNIDES

Printed in the United States of America
Corrected second printing, 2019

ISBN 978-0-9892536-7-3

www.PetroulisI@gmail.com

Author's Note

This book is the latest installment of my ongoing **Ex Cathedra** series that had its inception in the year 1972.

The present **Ex Cathedra** was written with the idea that its audience might be familiar with the author's previous work (the Magnum Opus *Amán Amán!* and **Ex Cathedras 9** through **23**).

Therefore, a few of the entries herein may not be understandable to a first-time reader.

Peter Joannides

December 1, 2014

Ex Cathedra

24th
Encyclical

von Herrn Doktor Professor Peter Joannides

1

I keep thinking of Dr. Lucius Hill: What he did for me; how he saved my life; how indebted to him I am.

Travel Hosts

The only ones I can stomach any longer are Burt Wolf and Rudy Maxa.

No more robots, goofballs, patronizers, self-promoters.

3

What disabuses me of solipsism more than anything else is the way other cars stop for red, and then, all together and instantly, rush forth on green.

4

Doctors, scientists, researchers… trying to make things better—only to be cancelled, negated, undone by polluters, profiteers, reverters…

All the more reason for a Planetary Dictatorship.

GOOD vs. EVIL

I never thought it would be so clearly instantiated.

DEMOCRATS vs. REPUBLICANS

Getting older and older is like fallen autumn leaves that begin to fade and turn brittle, and then crinklier and crinklier, and shriveled and more shriveled, until they become a powdery puff—and gone.

Timothy Garton Ash, "From the Lighthouse," **The New York Review of Books**, November 7, 2013, two and ¾ pages.

Here is a man who **HAS TOUCHED ALL THE BASES**, who has **NOT LEFT A STONE UNTURNED**. Such omnivorous reading and awareness (Noam Chomsky, Jean Paul Sartre, I.F. Stone, George Orwell, Václav Havel, J.M. Coetzee, Martin Heidegger, Barack Obama, Hillary Clinton, Isaiah Berlin, Hannah Arendt, David Riesman, Martin Luther King, President Kennedy, Malcolm Muggeridge, Petra Kelly, Nelson Mandela, Mark Mazower, Henri Bergson, Karl Marx,

(continued)

President Xi Jinping, Solzhenitsyn, Sakharov, Michnik, Aung San Suu Kyi, President Vladimir Putin, Marshal McLuhan, Gutenberg, De Gaulle, C.P. Scott), such a grasp of social currents and metamorphosing movements, such a breadth of knowledge and scholarship, such tying all the ends and loose ends together into a consistent and startling whole, such brilliance and wit ("Boris Pasternak not a writer? Heinrich Böll not a rebel?"), such a grasper of both long-past histories, and not long-past ones (Camelot), and even the very latest current events (Bo Xilai, Edward Snowden and the NSA), such a keeper abreast of happenings past, present, and to come.

The Universal and All-Encompassing Knower!

9

Red wine and blood: Two damnable things to get out of a fabric!

10

All those nasty things I said about actors and celebrities (whores) who do commercials.

But how can I forget that Alex used to do commercials?

11

How I've always wanted to take my friend Chuck, who is a painter, to Ikaria and, on a sunlit day, put him on the boat from Ayios Kirykos to Karkinagri.

Fred Thompson: Tennessean, politician, actor, commercial peddler.

With an accent almost as bad as that of Phil Gramm.

13

There's no end to editing, adjusting, fine-tuning, embellishing, refining, perfecting…

It can go on forever.

14

I'm beginning to feel considerable guilt about Connie.

And to a little lesser extent about Ninetta as well.

15

It's pretty obvious that **family** is the premier pivot and seal of human connectedness.

Mason G. Daly

A fine man, and certainly in his dealings with me.

Almost fired me during my Maryland stint, but didn't do so.

Arranged that I was sent to Iraklion, Crete on my first European assignment. (And then to Athens, Greece.)

Informed me I was welcome to rejoin Maryland after my hiatal hernia operation in the States.

I think of him with great respect and fondness.

17

There are times when one wishes to express his respect and fondness for another, only to find it to be too late to do so.

18

It pleases me considerably to learn this of Jonathan Swift: "He had little use for music, theater, opera, painting." (John Simon.)

19

The world of truckers: Far more interesting and intricate than academics have any inkling of.

20

When you get to know an irritating somebody, you sometimes find out he's not such a bad guy after all.

21

Sleeping all night in the same bed with someone is uncivilized.

22

Cartoon colors are so much more resplendent than those in real life.

23

I love to see the Greek flag come marching out first in the Olympics.

The best lines of **The Maltese Falcon**:

"When a man's partner is killed, he's supposed to do something about it. It doesn't make any difference what you thought of him. He was your partner and you're supposed to do something about it."

A very bad cold is as bad as anything can be.

Its only saving grace is that sooner or later it will cease to be.

26

It all began with Karaghiozi; and now (thanks to the Internet) it ends with Karaghiozi.

The open-ended vistas of youth are not one whit nullified by the closed-in strictures and doldrums of old age.

(See **Zarathustra,** "Reading and Writing")

Adam Gopnik

Oh, my, a man who's read everything, and knows everything, and, on top of it all, adds his cute and clever little twist to everything.

29

All those you've been mercilessly lambasting all
the time are really **television** (and print) personas. I
wonder what they might really be like if you got to know
them personally.

It isn't that Rachel Maddow is a lesbian; it's that she's a dyke.

Why do some writers cheapen everything they touch.

32

I don't like it when little puffed-up mousies talk

about Nietzsche,
                    flippantly.

33

I'm slowly getting to that accepting and understanding outlook of Inspector Maigret.

34

Joseph Rosendo, Travel Host

The worst sort of hubris, bar none.

Art Wolfe

Attend to the excellent photography.

Turn the audio off so that you don't have to suffer the inane homilies.

#'s 34 and 35

Joseph Rosendo and Art Wolfe, Travel Hosts

Joseph Rosendo is a Super-Jerk, and Art Wolfe is a jerk.

37

As soon as I get famous, it will be the exact time to stop writing.

Ex Cathedra 11, # 84

(Ex Cathedra 19, # 25; Ex Cathedra 22, # 168)

The hard choice: I guess it will have to be Barbara Rush.

Hydra, given the clutter of 2014, would be the **last** Greek island I would want to settle into.

40

A Terrible Thought

On August 12, 1985, 520 people perished on Japan Airlines Flight 123 because a riveting job was not properly done seven years earlier.

41

To Art Wolfe:

Did you ever consider making a documentary without you in it, or your outsize camera in it, or your slushy commentary and antics in it?

42

I think I would make a very good pilot,
NOW.

43

Shall I voice this utter heresy to myself?

I think I could accept, perhaps even like, a **certain** type of dog.

"Gentleman" Jim Jacobs

No one deserved the epithet more.

45

I am the center of my Universe, and also of the Universe-at-Large.

46

I don't think I can drive on the wrong (left) side of the road any longer; I am apt to cause an accident.

It's beginning to dawn on me, in the last few months or so, that every place is more or less like every other place.

The implications of this are staggering.

Why do so many doctors have (irritatingly) **Fox News** in their waiting rooms?

49

No more letters to old men!

Harold Bloom

Robert Silvers

John Simon

I know there is FAR FAR worse, but, in any case, here goes:

Top to Bottom
(and somewhere in between)

Continually balding, getting balder and balder. Daily light flashes on the side of left eye owing to a less-than-perfect cataract removal. Sunspots on my face that have to be frozen and treated. Memory lapses—cannot remember names of actors, friends, events, occasions that were once crystal-clear. Daily phlegm in my throat that threatens to choke me out of breathing, especially when lying supine. Every night, a dry mouth. Every so often a hacking cough in the morning. And as well a kitty-cat-like wheezing. Both shoulders shot to unholy hell. Trembling fingers. A lower back that screams at me every morning and sometimes the rest of the day, and a stooping posture. A bladder that won't quit—as many as ten nightly visits to a urinal. Neuropathy of the legs and so hardly any balance, short wobbly steps, and the indispensable cane. Telegrams from both knees and right hip: **Don't push it!** Swollen unsightly ankles. The periodic flare-ups of an inescapable gout. Unsightly fungoid toes.

And an ever more frequent general weakness and malaise.

And yet I carry on.

51

Please, God, deliver me from the Mercator Projection.

52

I like the thought of marrying your childhood sweetheart and living happily ever after.

When confronted with an ad, I know I am seeing **actors**.

Who are far removed from the earnestness and rapt emotings they project.

That's when the nausea settles in.

I feel such guilt watching, reading, dallying with fiction.

Kant's moral philosophy doesn't very much interest me, being inferior to that of Epicurus.

But his epistemology and ontology interest me greatly.

Thomas Wolfe and Peter Joannides

How can two people who differ so much in terms of background, pedigree, and habits—

have so much in common?

57

Mitch McConnell can't be all bad, now that I've seen his wife.

58

What is it about expats that I don't like?

I don't like old maps; they're inaccurate.

It's quite a jump, from one language to another.

61

All the once open spaces that used to be…

Now being gobbled up by obtruding obstructing overrunning structures.

62

Of all the Dead End Kids, I liked Huntz Hall the best, closely followed by Mahoney, the Malapropian.

63

Michael Palin is halfway there to Joseph Rosendo.

"Mia Trípa Sto Neró"

(Heraclitus and My Mother)

No matter how wide and varied the travel, it is but a mocking semblance of time, to be disannulled and supplanted by the ever-changing flux of things, with "new waters forever flowing upon you."

Book Signing

How can one sit at a table and offer her earnest and heartfelt "Hi!"s (with a little chit-chat at times thrown in) to scores and scores and scores of line-waiting patrons, one after another after another, and keep keeping up that artful politeness…

is something beyond my comprehension…

and beyond my approbation.

What people—aside from Greeks—do I feel the greatest **kinship** with?

Answer: Armenians.

When a celebrity does an ad, he or she immediately loses all sorts of points with me.

Protagoras and Immanuel Kant

Weren't they, in essence, saying the same thing?

69

Sex makes all of us a (Dr. Jekyll and) Mr. Hyde.

I haven't much interest in millionaires, or even low-end billionaires.

But up-end billionaires ($20 billion or more) is another matter!

71

I hear "The Tourist Industry"and I shudder.

How I miss the sweet and soothing narrator's voice of Phillip Hinton.

(In some strange way, he brings to mind the poet Ben Belitt.)

Without the heavy rain, **Rashomon** would not be the great film that it is.

In a National Election, an individual vote, considered individually, is **utterly** negligible with respect to its having any significant effect whatever. It will not change the outcome, undo trends and predictions, affect probabilities, redirect happenings... **Nothing** would turn out differently if it were not to be cast. It would only alter the final tally from, say, 65,918,507 to 65,918,506—one poor and lowly lonely crying digit.

A truly hard-nosed thinker might think hard about the implications of this.

Ex Cathedra 11, # 142

Now, I no longer even want a Seiko; a Timex will do me fine.

I hate what is done to children.

All over the world.

77

In a work of literature, spaces and geometrics
are as important as the words.

Great Men aren't so great, up close.

What is this "**I**" that is looking on, ever looking on? Looking on to my body hairs and splotchy nails and periodic pimples. Looking on to the accidents of my birth and place and circumstance. (I could have been a black man from Conakry or a brown man from Jakarta. ((Or even a stripèd zebra or colobus monkey.)) Or of a time in the 1920's or the 1880's.) What is this "**I**" that is looking on even in the midst of vicissitudes and pain (although it is hard to be looking on when in pain, and yet…)? What is this "**I**" that is looking on, ever looking on, removed in some strange way from all the many hazards and happenstances?

It's so hard for me to believe that lobsters were once the food of indentured servants and fed to prison inmates: a lowly food grudgingly eaten.

It is **very** hard for me to believe this.

81

I know I've said it before, and I know I have promised to avoid repetitions. But I cannot help it:

Planned obsolescence infuriates me!

The World of Art (Paintings)

I never could understand what the fuss is all about. For me, it is mostly an uninteresting subject.

Here's an interesting title:

Tourism, the Blight of the Planet

84

Sometimes I have queries about family and friends of old. Who married whom? What was the nephew's name? What country did his first cousin emigrate to?

And then to suddenly startlingly realize that there is no one around any longer to ask.

A Fond Memory

Back in Fork Union, while studying for our history class about the great Assyrian king Ashurbanipal, my roommate Boothby decides to christen him with the moniker "As You Bang on Your Balls."

80

Maybe it was the shoddy cooking and the absence of lemon and drawn butter.

I think I would find Prague **SUFFOCATING**.

I did some really really crazy things in my younger days.

I **wince** when I think about them.

I wait for the day when some celebrity—some Statesman, Royal, President, TV Anchor—starts the irreversible trend of not wearing a tie.

If I were an up-end billionaire, I'd be having weekly air shipments of wild partridges from Iran (Nero?) and fresh apricots from Armenia.

Easy to lambast strangers.

Harder to do so with people you know.

No people age more gracelessly than Americans.

93

It gladdens my soul that the great forest and primeval swampland of Okefenokee is so close nearby.

94

All sorts of things make me almost break down.

What sort of Planetary Dictator am I to be if I'm always on the verge of breaking down?

The wonder of physics: raindrops wiggling down a windshield.

Some Brits are pretentious, self-important, and stupid.

Like Paul Strathern who calls **Zarathustra**, probably one of the greatest works of philosophy and literature, "simplistic," "unbearable bombast," "pearl of unwisdom," "unreadable."

An arrogant toad.

I defend my authors, **Vehemently**.

98

There's no point in telling those who are retarded, that they're retarded.

99

And yet more considerable guilt: my son in Greece.

100

And yet still more considerable guilt: what I've
put Nona through.

The difference between a BBC and an American documentary having to do with any serious and interesting subject is that the American one invariably has to jazz it up a bit.

APA Meeting (Eastern Division Program)

Registration, Chairs, Speakers, Commentators, Colloquia, Group Session IV, Group Meetings 5:15-7:15...

My God! do things like this still go on?

Bodyguards who would assassinate their charges: Presidents, Prime Ministers, Commanders…

What a perverted, aberrant note.

Sometimes when I think of science, engineering, invention, technology… I suspect that I and all my artsy fellow-travelers may very well be frauds.

105

I wonder if it ever crosses the mind of Professors of Philosophy, English, Humanities, the Arts... that they may have never really earned their salaries.

I don't like to share my living space with anything that flies, buzzes, creeps, slithers, wriggles, crawls—or just plain **MOVES**.

From now on I've decided to call my **Sub Specie Aeterni** moments my **Lackawanna 16356** moments, in honor of Thomas Wolfe.

108

Thugs, all over the world: Italian thugs, Russian thugs, American thugs.

But I'll bet there are no Laplander thugs or Falklander thugs.

What prisons need is a little greenery.

Some people are just **pinched**.

That's the only word for it.

111

The aliens are among us: jellyfish.

112

Bits and pieces, elusive wisps and wraiths of memory sometimes come wafting back, but I can't, for the life of me, remember where or when or what.

113

Sickness, disease, pain: how trivial everything
else seems when confronted with these.

114

Small first-rate hotels in arresting and out-of-the-

way locations,
                instead of glitzy behemoths.

115

Eskimo huskies: the only truly handsome dogs.

116

Parabola

The rapid stages of babies/ The rapid stages of old men.

I just now learn things about places I have visited that I had no idea about when I visited them.

(Example: The Golden Temple of Amritsar.)

118

It really is refreshing to hear Bill Maher tell it like it is.

119

After all these years, another aesthetic epiphany, to be added to the handful already stumbled upon:

The onset of dusk, sitting comfortably outdoors at the Town Center, sipping red wine, and looking up to suddenly see fading white clouds drifting through a sky of periwinkle blue.

Thugs: wild animals without the dignity of wild animals.

121

What happened to the days when my passport
had **five** extra series of pages attached, full of stamps,
notations, and visas, and would open and flutter in the
breeze like an accordion.

I hate being patronized by two-bit academic snots.

.

123

What a frightening and yet exhilarating thought:
to disavow all my previous opinions.

122

As well as two-bit editorial and publishing snots.

The other day the wheel assembly of a large truck going southbound on I-95 came loose, went over the median, and crashed into a northbound car, killing the driver.

I can't imagine a more unalloyed case of winning the lottery in reverse.

State Senator John Thrasher, "elected" to be President of Florida State University.

That "Good Ol' Boy" network of the Deep South still alive and kicking, still rearing its dismal head.

127

Given the dangers involved, I never could understand the fascination with speleology.

When I was 7, 8, 9, 10, 11, 12, living out my unsullied boyhood in New York/New Jersey, the horrible things that were happening in the world, at the same time.

It sickens me when Westerners patronize the natives.

130

"**Deep down inside,** he's really a good man," doesn't really cut it, does it?

Come the Revolution, to be outlawed forthwith!

Boxing

NASCAR

Football

Rugby

Larry King is now doing commercials.

I would have thought that after all the years of raking in enough money to build a stupendous Saudi harem, such a pursuit wouldn't be necessary.

Somewhere in my writing, I used the milder Greek word to describe him and, deliberately, so as not to offend.

I am now prepared, and unapologetically, to use the harsher English word instead.

133

Surely torture has to be the most inexcusable, the most evil, the most heinous, vicious, vile thing on earth.

134

If I weren't who I am, I would like to have been an etymologist or an anthropologist/archeologist.

Or maybe a paleontologist.

So much talk of evolution makes it sound as if animals **strive** to evolve, a kind of thrusting, reaching, active process, when, as I understand it, it is really a matter of differential rates of reproduction governed by surrounding circumstances, and thus quite a passive process.

I wouldn't want to tangle with a chimp or baboon.

I have found two mistakes in my **Magnum Opus**: a superfluous "l" in a transliterated Greek word, and a lower case "o" that should have been capitalized.

I am devastated.

Despite all its overwhelming advantages, you have no idea how hard it has been for an old typewriter hand to get used to the computer.

139

One of the boons of modern technology: After thousands and thousands (millions) of years, finally no more head lice and also no more pubic lice.

140

The other day I happened to catch Bill O'Reilly, and, would you believe it, he actually made good sense!

The times and summers in Rhodos, now that years have elapsed, have suddenly become as nostalgic and hallowed as any earlier sylphs and memories…

have suddenly become treasured and inviolate.

What in the world did I have in common with myself when I was 17? When I was 35? When I was 50?...

143

Religions are like tattoo parlors.

Can you make the connection?

144

It's happening more and more frequently: When I watch TV, I just look at the pictures and turn the volume way way low until it's just a barely understandable murmur.

I now travel, not to see new things, for there are no new things, but just to be **stimulated** by the kaleidoscope of old things.

All my life I've been full of instant likes and dislikes (people).

Maybe I should get over it.

(Although I'm not sure I should.)

I remember as a boy, Mama would talk about Ungó, the great French writer Ungó.

It was only years later that I realized she was speaking of Victor Hugo.

I can't abide fiction anymore.

I'd **so** much rather watch a documentary.

131

I am considering, as well:

Soccer

Ice Hockey

128

Horrible things happening—at the same time.

Not just between 1938 and 1943—but all of the time.

151

Two Teams

Going hell-bent against one another.

You have absolutely no bias or connection to either one and are totally disinterested.

In not too short a time, you will invariably be pulling for one over the other.

152

I think I could learn how to speak the language
of the Kalahari Bushmen before I could learn how to
speak French.

153

Ham 'n eggs.

Nero 'n orchids.

If you were to win $100,000,000 **clear** in the Mega Lotto, you could give $100,000 to each of 150 individuals (family and friends), and pay all relevant gift taxes, and still be left with enough money to invest at a 4% return and, without disturbing the principal, have a yearly income of nearly $2,000,000 **after taxes**.

Every night we dream.

We just cannot every time remember.

There is no way to **directly** verify this.

(All the brain studies are suggestive, but irrelevant.)

Nevertheless, I still think it's true.

156

What a wonderful liberation: to be free of the grappling hook of sex!

157

How moving and heartening it is to see white people, black people, brown people, Orientals dining together, playing together, kibitzing together, helping one another, casually and unmindful of their physical differences.

And only in the USA is this a truly genuine thing.

All those smart-asses who use untranslated French phrases in their articles.

I'm now paying them back in my **Ex Cathedras** with my untranslated Greek.

159

I rather liked Captain Sankara of Burkina Faso, I know not why, so I'm glad Blaise Compaoré is now getting his.

My instincts are better than many another's analyses.

It's always amusing when a parent, puffy-proud and beaming, cheerily announces:

"I have 7 children, 24 grandchildren and 2 great-grandchildren."

Shouldn't there be a certain amount of guilt involved?

I always felt intimidated by native-born Greeks who spoke the language well.

I wish I were like my friend Cyrus who would let the city-slickers of Athens have it with his atrocious broken Greek, always made his point, and couldn't have cared less.

Fascism is correct.

It's just that we've had bad fascists.

To tell the truth, it's **insulting** to be urged to vote.

I'm not some sort of collective cog in some collective machine that must stand up and perform.

A Version of Hell

When the names of all geographical places are replaced by numbers.

I shall never forget the shores of Lago Enriquillo in the Dominican Republic.

A landscape that looked utterly groomed and artificial, when in fact it was utterly natural.

 # 49

And no more palavers with Chairs of English Departments!

University of North Florida

Florida State University

168

No poetic line has ever invaded and imprisoned my brain more than so:

"O lost, and by the wind grieved, ghost, come back again."

169

The French sound like Thanksgiving turkeys gobble-gobble-gobbling at one another.

I've given up on all Instructional Manuals.

171

Money earned from one's writing is dirty money.

The most honorable way to make money is to win the Lotto.

173

Jonathan Miller speaks so well, that it's a pleasure to hear him talk about—anything whatever.

174

I'm glad so many are so inventive and industrious.

Because I am so profoundly, metaphysically, lazy.

What is this utter nonsense about "Don't go to bed right after eating."

176

I've never been very good at putting myself in someone else's place.

177

The very first song, in English, that I remember:

"South of the border♪, down Mexico way♫"

It was hell having to catch a baseball with a left-hand mitt, then yank off the mitt and put it under my right armpit as lightning fast as I could, and then throw the ball as hard as I could to get the runner out.

"The stars at night are big and bright♪

(clap, clap, clap, clap, clap)

Deep in the heart of Texas♫"

How sweet the thought of Texas then, how warm and familial and proprietary.

And how ill-disposed the thought of Texas now—alien and offensive and irritating me no end.

Oh all those hours and hours and hours spent in the library, querying librarians, looking things up, rummaging in the stacks…

When I could have been in my pajamas at home, with a coffee or drink, getting all the info on Google.

181

I know it's the civilized and rational and equitable thing to do, but I still strongly resent having to wait for a red light.

Three noteworthy Greeks: Jim Londos, the wrestler; Koutalianos, the Strongman; Nick the Greek, the Gambler.

I used to rant at Jones College Stereo 90.9 (Jacksonville, Florida) for what I considered to be too many interruptions and solicitations.

Then the station was sold.

And now I miss terribly the soft soothing music.

And am saddled with the unmitigated garbage that replaced it.

As a kid (and even to this day) I always feared the undersides of wrists.

All those blood vessels and embrangling crisscrossing veins and capillaries and their soft vulnerability.

I would shudder, start to feel weak, and go limp.

185

I never could have made a doctor or a lawyer or a politician or an Ambassador or a General or an Entertainer or an Actor or a Pundit…

I probably would have made a good Accountant.

187

I am where I belong.

188

How cozy/comfy it is to sit in my la-z-boy recliner with my big wide TV monitor screen and watch the traffic snarls and seething manswarms of Bangkok, Delhi, Cairo, Lagos, São Paulo…

189

If you're going to reverse a referee's call on the basis of high-tech cameras, then why have a referee at all?

I don't think an accent is a superficial thing.

That cursèd **Magnum Opus** has been a monkey on my back since 1958.

Madrassas with their mindless bobbing ba-bobbing children's heads do thoroughly depress and disconcert me.

193

It's beginning to dawn on me that so many have had a grim childhood.

I don't think I've ever been to a lovelier place than the Valley of Swat in Pakistan.

195

Corruption, of necessity, sets in—the instant one becomes famous.

I haven't thought about Henry Miller in a long long time.

His sway with me was strong and incisive and pronounced.

Dare I, dare I, now be a bit critical?

Some thoughts, memories, experiences are so privately enshrouded and enmeshed, they really can't be written about.

198

He who lives the longest: the picaresque traveler.

There was a restaurant at Zephiros, Rhodos that would serve freshly-caught whole octopus with all its tentacles there and intact, abundant lemons, **fresh** potatoes freshly-cut and fried, **vlíta**, and a bottle of CAIR retsina.

Who could ask for anything more.

And then there was the seaside taverna at Tragano Beach: **marithákia** crunched and swallowed whole, abundant lemons, **patátes tiyanités, horiátiki saláta, biftéki, vlíta,** a bottle of CAIR retsina—and the pebbly beach with its cool and limpid waters just a stone's throw away.

www.ingramcontent.com/pod-product-compliance
Lightning Source LLC
Chambersburg PA
CBHW071959040426
42447CB00009B/1406